Festivals *of the* World

SAUDI ARABIA

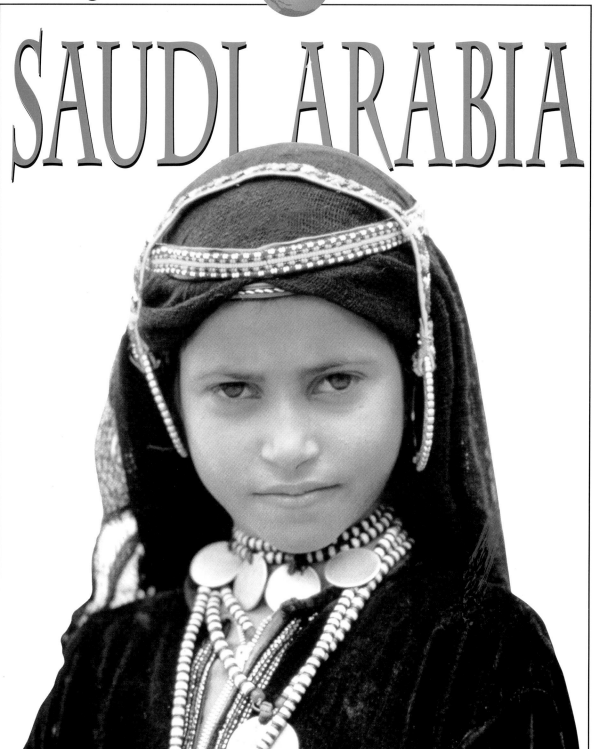

Gareth Stevens Publishing
MILWAUKEE

Written by
MARIA O'SHEA

Edited by
KEN CHANG

Designed by
HASNAH MOHD ESA

Picture research by
SUSAN JANE MANUEL

First published in North America in 1999 by
Gareth Stevens Publishing
1555 North RiverCenter Drive, Suite 201
Milwaukee, Wisconsin 53212 USA

For a free color catalog describing Gareth
Stevens' list of high-quality books and multimedia
programs, call
1-800-542-2595 (USA)
or 1-800-461-9120 (Canada).
Gareth Stevens Publishing's Fax: (414) 225-0377.

© TIMES EDITIONS PTE LTD 1999
Originated and designed by
Times Books International
an imprint of Times Editions Pte Ltd
Times Centre, 1 New Industrial Road
Singapore 536196
Printed in Malaysia

Library of Congress Cataloging-in-Publication Data:
O'Shea, Maria.
Saudi Arabia / by Maria O'Shea.
p. cm. — (Festivals of the world)
Includes bibliographical references and index.
Summary: Describes how the culture of Saudi
Arabia is reflected in its many festivals, including
Eid el-Fitr, Eid el-Adha, and the Jinadriyah
National Festival.
ISBN 0-8368-2026-6 (lib. bdg.)
1. Festivals—Saudi Arabia—Juvenile literature.
2. Saudi Arabia—Social life and customs—
Juvenile literature. 3. Saudi Arabia—Religious life
and customs—Juvenile literature. [1. Festivals—
Saudi Arabia. 2. Holidays—Saudi Arabia.
3. Saudi Arabia—Social life and customs.]
I. Title. II. Series.
GT4874.5.S33085   1999
394.26962—dc21   99-10656

1 2 3 4 5 6 7 8 9 03 02 01 00 99

CONTENTS

It's Festival Time . . .

In Saudi Arabia, festivals are known as *Eids* [eeds]. An Eid is a special celebration of religion and family. It is a time to pray, feast, give thanks, visit friends and relatives, and exchange gifts. Although there are only two Eids celebrated by Saudi Arabians each year, Eid el-Fitr [eed el-FIT-ter] and Eid el-Adha [eed el-AHD-ha], there are many other events Saudi Arabians like to celebrate! It's festival time in Saudi Arabia . . .

WHERE'S SAUDI ARABIA?

Saudi Arabia is the largest nation in the Middle East, a region where the continents of Europe, Africa, and Asia meet. It occupies 80 percent of the Arabian Peninsula. Saudi Arabia is an extremely dry country, with much of the land made up of scorching hot rock or sandy desert.

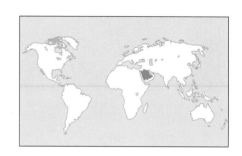

Under the rocks and sand lie the biggest oil reserves in the world, which have made the Saudi Arabians extremely wealthy.

Who are the Saudi Arabians?

The first Saudi Arabians were the Bedouins [BED-oo-ins], or "desert people," who wandered from place to place in search of pastures for their herds of sheep and camels. Since the discovery of oil, most Saudi Arabians have let go of their traditional way of life and have settled in the cities. The people are strongly united by **Islam**, the official religion of Saudi Arabia. All **Muslims** think of Saudi Arabia as the birthplace and home of Islam.

This smiling Saudi Arabian boy wears a white headdress to keep cool in the sun.

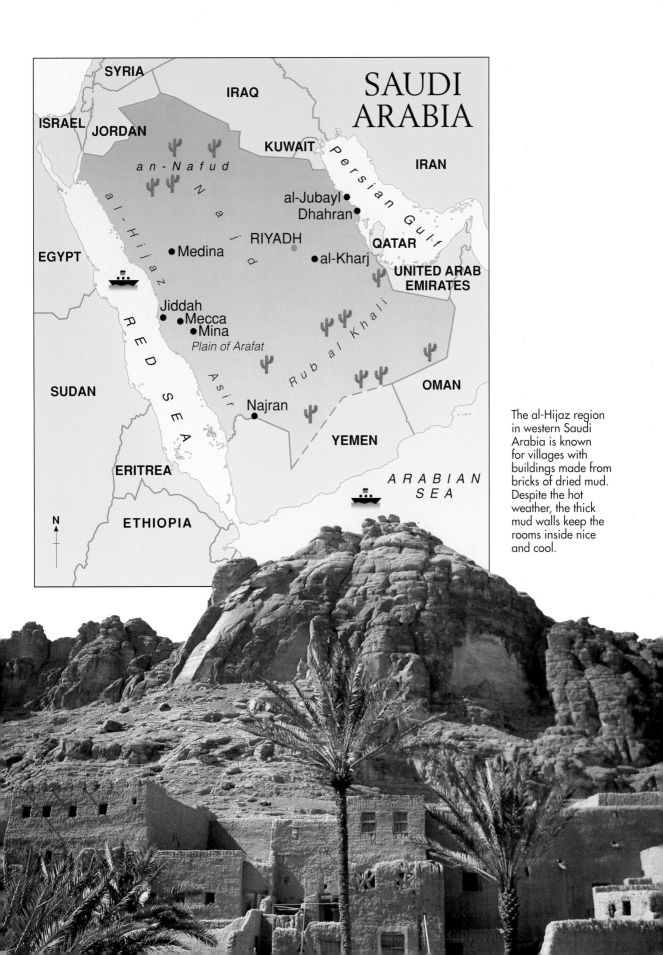

SAUDI ARABIA

SYRIA

IRAQ

ISRAEL

JORDAN

KUWAIT

IRAN

an-Nafud

al-Jubayl ●
Dhahran ●

Persian Gulf

EGYPT

N a j d

Medina ●

RIYADH ●

QATAR

al-Kharj ●

UNITED ARAB
EMIRATES

al-Hijaz

Jiddah
● Mecca
● Mina
Plain of Arafat

Rub al Khali

SUDAN

Asir

Najran ●

OMAN

RED SEA

ERITREA

YEMEN

*ARABIAN
SEA*

ETHIOPIA

N

The al-Hijaz region
in western Saudi
Arabia is known
for villages with
buildings made from
bricks of dried mud.
Despite the hot
weather, the thick
mud walls keep the
rooms inside nice
and cool.

WHEN'S THE EID?

Saudi Arabian holidays follow the Islamic **lunar** calendar, which has 12 months. Each month starts with the new moon. Sometimes the new moon isn't clear at night, making it difficult to predict the exact start of a Muslim holiday. The Islamic calendar year is 354 days, while the Gregorian calendar year is 365 days. This difference means that the dates of Muslim holidays change each year on the Gregorian calendar. For some non-religious holidays, Saudi Arabians follow the Gregorian calendar. Keeping track of time on two different calendars is not always easy!

ISLAMIC CALENDAR HOLIDAYS

- ✪ **ISLAMIC NEW YEAR**—The first day of the Islamic calendar marks the time in the year A.D. 622 when Prophet Muhammad, the founder of Islam, fled from the city of Mecca.
- ✪ **BIRTH OF THE PROPHET**—The birthday of Prophet Muhammad.
- ✪ **RAMADAN**—A spiritual occasion when Muslims fast from dawn to dusk for 30 days.
- ✪ **EID EL-FITR**—The most important festival in Islam, when Muslims celebrate the end of the Ramadan fast.
- ✪ **THE HAJJ**—Every year, Muslims from many countries gather in Mecca, the most sacred Islamic city, for six days of prayer and worship.
- ✪ **EID EL-ADHA**—A celebration of thanksgiving during the hajj.

GREGORIAN CALENDAR HOLIDAYS

Saudi Arabian festivals are for both young and old. Come join us!

- ✪ **JINADRIYAH NATIONAL FESTIVAL**—A traditional arts festival for poets, dancers, musicians, and craftsmen.
- ✪ **SAUDI NATIONAL DAY**—Every year on September 23rd, Saudi Arabians celebrate the founding of the Kingdom of Saudi Arabia in 1932 by Abdul Aziz ibn Saud.

RAMADAN

R amadan [rah-mah-DAHN] is the holiest month of the Islamic calendar. It celebrates the founding of Islam, when Prophet Muhammad received the sacred words of the **Qur'an** [kor-AHN] from the Angel Gabriel.

For 30 days, Muslims do not eat or drink between sunrise and sunset. Muslims believe that fasting makes a stronger and better person. Fasting teaches people to control their bodies, to know the feeling of hunger, and to appreciate God's gift of food. Not everyone fasts. The elderly, the sick, children, and pregnant women do not have to fast. Besides fasting, Muslims pray often during Ramadan. Families recite the Qur'an for 45 minutes each evening. By the end of Ramadan, they have recited the entire holy book.

The evening **iftar** [EEF-tar] table is set with delicious fruits, dates, breads, and salads.

These children are enjoying a meal during Ramadan. Although they are not expected to fast, even small children will try fasting for a day or more to practice for when they are older.

Changing a daily routine

Ramadan is very different from a normal "holiday." For 30 days, Muslims must change their lifestyle and their sense of daily time. Children go to school for only a few hours during Ramadan. Shops stay closed during the day and do not open until late at night. People sleep for much of the day, then spend their evenings praying, feasting, and visiting friends—sometimes until dawn!

During Ramadan, Muslims eat in the dark. Every morning before sunrise, they enjoy the *sohour* [SO-hore], which is a wholesome meal of meat, rice, and bread. They must eat a lot in the morning, or they will get too hungry while fasting during the day. The evening meal, called iftar, is a rewarding feast of fruits, soups, meats, and sweets.

Men and women pray at a **mosque** in the holy city of Mecca in western Saudi Arabia. Prayer is as much a part of Ramadan as fasting.

Above: The Prophet's Mosque stands in Medina, the second most sacred city after Mecca.

The Night of Power

Prophet Muhammad received the first scriptures of the Qur'an on one of the last 10 nights of Ramadan. Muslims call this night *Lailat-ul Qadr* [lye-LAH-tul ka-DAHR], or the Night of Power. Because no one knows exactly which of the 10 nights is the Night of Power, Muslims usually become particularly devoted to religion throughout the end of Ramadan, to be certain of catching the exact day of Muhammad's **revelation**. Some Muslims even spend all of the last 10 nights of Ramadan at prayer in the mosques. Ramadan festivities also intensify at this time. Bedouins in the desert might beat drums all night long.

Opposite: This iftar feast is outside a mosque. When the sun has set and the fast is over, it's time to eat and make new friends.

Think about this

Imagine not eating or drinking for 18 hours in the blazing heat of the Saudi Arabian summer! All Saudi Arabians are grateful when Ramadan falls in the winter season. For Saudi Arabians living in non-Muslim countries, Ramadan is especially difficult because most of the people around them do not fast. How would you feel if everyone around you was eating, but you had to fast for the entire day?

EID EL-FITR

As Ramadan draws to a close, Saudi Arabians look eagerly into the night sky to catch sight of the crescent moon that signals the start of the new month. If the new moon is sighted, the festival of Eid el-Fitr will be celebrated the following night. If the moon does not appear clearly, the festival might be delayed an extra day. News of the moon over Mecca is spread all over the world, so all Muslims can celebrate on the same day. Eid el-Fitr means "Feast of the Breaking of the Fast."

Saudi Arabian children have lots to do on Eid el-Fitr. They wear new clothes, visit relatives, receive gifts, go on picnics, paint pictures, and eat many delicious foods. No wonder they enjoy this festival so much!

This pretty little girl is dressed up in her new Eid clothes, ready for feasting, fun—and presents!

The fast ends, the feast begins

On the last night of Ramadan, hungry families gather for a special meal of their favorite foods. The end of the fast puts everyone in a happy mood. The next morning, families rise very early and dress in new clothes made specially for this day. Then they gather at the mosque for the Eid prayer. In this prayer, Muslims give thanks to God because, without his help, they would never have made it through Ramadan. After the Eid prayer, families prepare for the evening's feasting and festivities!

Look at these fancy sweetmeats! Eid el-Fitr is the most elaborate feast of the year. Imagine what your appetite would be like after fasting for 30 days!

Outdoor fun

Muslims spend much of Eid el-Fitr indoors—at home, cooking for the feast; at friends' homes, enjoying tea and sweets; or at the mosque for prayer—but there is much to see and do outdoors, too. Saudi Arabians decorate streets and buildings with fairy lights and paintings. Families go to fun fairs and amusement parks, or find a nice spot for a relaxing picnic. Since there are few public holidays in Saudi Arabia, families like to travel around the time of Eid el-Fitr, either overseas or to the mountain resorts near Mecca. Some families camp out in the desert, as the Bedouins do, to enjoy nature.

This family has traveled to the Saudi Arabian coast on Eid el-Fitr to have a picnic.

Gifts for all

During Ramadan, people shop for gifts and cards to exchange with family and friends on Eid el-Fitr. Saudi Arabians like to get money as gifts, so the banks are very busy the day before the Eid.

Eid el-Fitr is also a time for being generous to the needy. Every family donates money (the cost of one meal for each member of the family) to the mosque. The donations are then passed on to the poor. All Muslims—old, young, rich, or poor—enjoy a happy Eid.

Left: On Eid el-Fitr, Muslims give out colorful Eid cards. You can learn how to make one on page 28.

Think about this

Looking forward to a big festival at the end of Ramadan helps Saudi Arabians endure fasting, but, sometimes, parents will also promise their children special gifts if they can manage to fast, even for a day. Do you think you could fast for 30 days if you knew there would be a big celebration after the last day?

These children are helping their mother prepare special foods for the Eid feast. On Eid el-Fitr, all Muslims feel they have a duty to serve their families and communities.

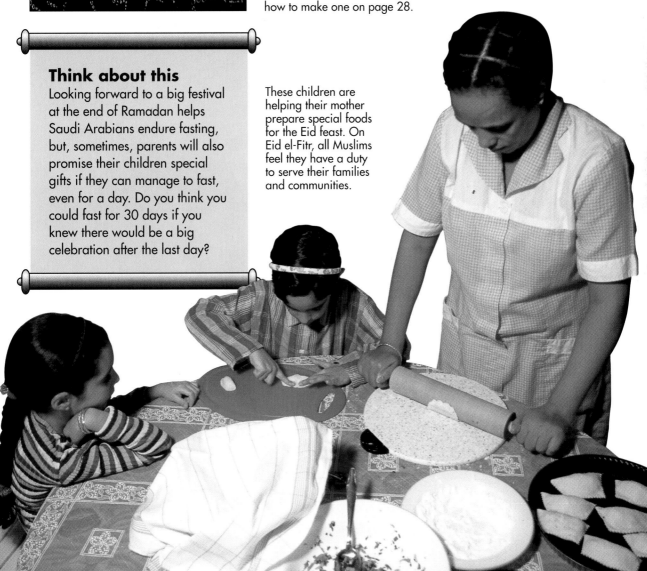

THE HAJJ

Two months after Eid el-Fitr, the hajj [HAHJ] begins. The hajj is a yearly **pilgrimage** that every Muslim must try to make at least once in his or her lifetime. Every year, over two million Muslims from all over the world come to the city of Mecca for the hajj. They travel by land, sea, and air to take part in a series of ancient, sacred **rituals**. Like fasting during Ramadan, the hajj is considered a "pillar of Islam," which means that it is a very important duty for Muslims to perform.

These young pilgrims will go to Mecca for the hajj. Hajj pilgrims are of all ages.

The Holy City of Mecca

Mecca is the birthplace of Prophet Muhammad, so it is the holiest city in Islam. Only Muslims can enter the city.

The Grand Mosque of Mecca is big enough to hold almost one million worshipers! In the center of the mosque stands the **Ka'bah** [KAH-bah], the shrine all Muslims face when praying. During the six days of the hajj, the Saudi Arabian government provides food, water, shelter, transportation, and hospitals for all the hajj pilgrims staying in Mecca. Imagine trying to house and feed two million people, many of whom do not even speak a common language!

Above: Pilgrims surround the Ka'bah on the first and last day of the hajj.

Below: These women are praying during the hajj.

17

In Mina, pilgrims throw stones at three stone pillars. The stones represent evil. By throwing the stones, the pilgrims rid themselves of evil.

Rituals of the hajj

When entering Mecca for the hajj, men must dress in simple white gowns, and women must keep their faces unveiled. All pilgrims should appear equal before God. On the first day of the hajj, pilgrims enter the Grand Mosque and walk around the Ka'bah seven times. The most important ceremony of the hajj is "The Standing" on the Plain of Arafat, southeast of Mecca, where pilgrims spend the entire day in prayer. After the festival of Eid el-Adha, on the third day of the hajj, the pilgrims walk to the town of Mina for the "stoning of the pillars," a ritual that cleanses them of evil. They return to Mecca for a final circling of the Ka'bah on the last day of the hajj.

Below: During the hajj, Muslims live in a city of tents and pray often.

The journey home

Each hajj pilgrim returns home from Mecca as a *hajji* [HAHJ-ee], or a Muslim who has completed the pilgrimage. It isn't easy, however, to get home when millions of people are trying to leave the same city at the same time. Hajjis often stay in Mecca for a while, until the crowd has gone. Just before they leave, they perform a final circling of the Ka'bah.

Since most Muslims can afford to perform the hajj only once in their lifetimes, many hajjis also visit the Prophet's tomb in Medina after their pilgrimage to Mecca. Medina is another holy city of Islam, north of Mecca. Prophet Muhammad was born in Mecca and died in Medina.

These hajjis are heading home. Pilgrims usually arrive in and depart from the city of Jiddah.

Think about this

A long time ago, it took many years to reach Mecca by foot, ship, or camel caravan. The journey was so long that many people never completed the hajj because they were too old, sick, or poor. Muslims who die during their pilgrimage to Mecca are treated as if they had successfully arrived, and, afterward, they are thought of as hajjis.

19

EID EL-ADHA

E id el-Adha, or "Feast of the Sacrifice," commemorates Prophet Ibrahim's great sacrifice for God. Although Eid el-Adha falls during the hajj, it is a festival for all Muslims, not just pilgrims. It is a time for prayer, sacrifice, sharing, and feasting.

The Prophet Ibrahim

Muslims believe the Prophet Ibrahim (the Muslim name for Abraham) lived in what is now Saudi Arabia. Ibrahim's son Ismail was born near Mecca. As a test of faith, God ordered Ibrahim to make a fire and offer his son Ismail as a sacrifice. Ibrahim was committed to obeying God's command, so he took his son to the altar. As Ibrahim was about to slay Ismail, God saved Ismail from his father's knife and made Ibrahim sacrifice a sheep instead. Later, Ismail helped Ibrahim build the Ka'bah, a place in Mecca dedicated to the worship of God.

Street children look forward to Eid el-Adha, when kind Muslims share with the poor meat from the animals they sacrifice.

Sacrifice and giving

To remind themselves of Ibrahim's willingness to serve God, Muslims sacrifice an animal on Eid el-Adha, the second most important festival after Eid el-Fitr. They give a third of the meat to the poor, a third to their friends, and keep a third for their families. A really kind Muslim will buy an animal for a poor family so they can take part in the sacrifice, too. For days before Eid el-Adha, Mecca and other Saudi Arabian cities are full of animals waiting to be sold. Saudi Arabia imports more than six million live sheep each year, most of which will be sacrificed on this day. Traditionally, the animals are decorated with red **henna** and decorative bridles before the sacrifice.

Above: Pilgrims celebrate Eid el-Adha with a feast.

Below: On Eid el-Adha, pilgrims sacrifice sheep. Can you see the henna marks on the sheep that have been picked to be sacrificed?

Above: After the sacrifice comes the feast. This tasty Arabian dish is made with lamb and rice.

Think about this
Many of the stories from the Qur'an are familiar to Jews and Christians. Muslims believe that Islam is not a new religion, but the final, complete version of Judaism and Christianity. Jesus Christ and all the prophets of the Old Testament are accepted as prophets by Muslims.

A festival to give thanks

All Muslims visit the mosque on the morning of Eid el-Adha to offer a special prayer. Then, everyone visits family and friends, arriving with trays of fresh meat from the sacrifice. Adults bring sweets and gifts for the children. In the evening, families enjoy elaborate meals, featuring meat from the sacrifice at the center of the table. All Muslims, rich or poor, eat heartily. The mosque donates meat to families who cannot afford it.

Right: Eid el-Adha is a festival for families to spend time together. These boys and their father live in Najran, a city near the Rub al Khali Desert.

Opposite: Eids are religious festivals, so attending the mosque for prayer and worship is very important.

23

JINADRIYAH NATIONAL FESTIVAL

Every year, in February, over one million Saudi Arabians have a chance to see how their ancestors lived. Under the patronage of the king of Saudi Arabia, the National Guard organizes a two-week festival at what has become a permanent heritage village in the middle of the desert.

Why celebrate the past?

Saudi Arabia has undergone many incredible changes in the last 50 years. Modernization has happened so fast that many Saudi Arabians have lost touch with the lifestyles of the past. The Jinadriyah [jin-ah-DREE-uh] Festival allows both children and adults to learn about their nation's ancient heritage.

This folk musician is playing a tune that has been passed down over many centuries.

Festive Arabian traditions

Above: Look at the beautiful costumes of these ardha dancers.

The Jinadriyah Festival opens with an exciting and noisy camel race. Folklore troupes perform the *ardha* [AHR-duh], the national dance of Saudi Arabia. The ardha is a traditional sword dance that combines singing, dancing, and poetry. Men carrying swords stand shoulder to shoulder and dance in a circle, while a poet sings and drummers beat out a rhythm. The festival also has a poetry reading competition, folk music concerts, and craft workshops.

The well-disciplined Saudi Arabian National Guards watch over the Jinadriyah Festival.

THINGS FOR YOU TO DO

Weddings are very festive occasions in Saudi Arabia. Before every wedding, the bride takes part in a henna ceremony in which the female guests paint pretty patterns on the bride's hands with henna. Henna is a strong dye that fades very slowly. Hennaed hands are a sign of both good luck and happiness, so some women henna their hands to celebrate other occasions. You do not need an occasion to henna your hands. With your parent's permission, you can try it now!

Make henna paste

First, you need to buy henna, which is a green powder. You can buy it at oriental stores, health food stores, and cosmetic suppliers. Ask for the natural red color. Mix about one cup of henna with enough water to make a thin paste (the consistency of poster paint). The paste will be dark green in color, but it will leave a red-orange stain on your skin.

Let's paint!

When the henna paste is ready, it's time to decorate your hands. You will need some old dishcloths, the henna paste, a small paintbrush, a lemon, and a friend. Wash and dry your hands. Place your hands on a table. Cover the table with dishcloths so you don't accidentally stain it. Then have your friend paint your hands with the henna paste using a paintbrush. Usually, henna artists will paint thinly lined patterns on the fingers and back of the hands and coat the palms and pads of the fingers. Your friend might try painting simple flowers or curling spirals. What patterns do you like?

When your friend has finished painting, squeeze lemon juice over each hand and let your hands dry. Lemon juice keeps the dye from smearing. Then wrap each hand in a clean dishcloth and wait for at least half an hour. (While a Saudi Arabian bride waits, the wedding guests will sing and dance to entertain her. They also feed her because she can't use her hands!) Rinse your hands under running water, and you're finished. Go celebrate with your lucky, hennaed hands! The henna will fade every time you wash your hands.

Things to look for in your library

Fasting During Ramadan. (Islamic Information Services, 1994).
Hajj: The Fifth Pillar of Islam. (Islamic Information Services, 1994).
Saudi Arabia. Leila Merrill Foster (Childrens Press, 1993).
Saudi Arabia, a Country Study. Helen Metz (U.S. Government Printing Office, 1993).
Saudi Arabia in Pictures. (Lerner Publications, 1990).
The Saudis: Inside the Desert Kingdom. Sandra Mackey (Hodder and Stoughton, 1990).
Welcome to Saudi Arabia. (http://darkwing.uoregon.edu/~kbatarfi/saudi.html).

MAKE AN EID CARD

On Eid el-Fitr, Muslims enjoy making special cards to exchange with family and friends. Children always rush to open their cards because the cards might contain money as a gift! Try making an Eid card for a friend or someone in your family. You can even learn how to write a greeting on the card in the Arabic language!

You will need:
1. A piece of cardboard or construction paper, 8 ½" x 11" (22 x 28 cm)
2. Paints
3. Paint tray
4. Gold marker
5. Black marker
6. Pencil
7. Paintbrushes

1 Fold the cardboard in half. In Arabic, you read from right to left, so cards open the opposite way English ones do. Sketch a design on the front of the card.

2 Color in the design with paints and gold marker. Blue, green, gold, and silver are the most popular colors in Islamic decorations.

عيد سعيد

3 Inside the card, write "*Eid Sa'id*" (EED say-eed), which means "Happy Festival." You can write it in Arabic, too. Just outline the Arabic script above in pencil, then fill it in using black marker. Now you can give your Eid card to a friend. Happy Festival!

29

Make Khoshaf

D uring Ramadan, everyone waits patiently for sunset so they can break the fast with the evening meal, or iftar. *Khoshaf* [koe-SHAAF], a snack of sweetened fruits, is often served as an iftar dish in Saudi Arabia. Of course, you don't have to fast to enjoy khoshaf. You just need to be hungry!

You will need:

1. A saucepan
2. 1 cup (240 milliliters) of water
3. 2 ounces (57 grams) mixed nuts
4. 4 ounces (114 g) dried prunes
5. 2 ounces (57 g) mixed dried fruits
6. 2 dried figs, chopped
7. A mixing bowl
8. 3 ounces (85 g) raisins
9. Plain yogurt
10. ¼ teaspoon ground nutmeg
11. 2 cinnamon sticks
12. 8 ounces (227 g) dried apricots
13. 2 tablespoons sugar
14. Wooden spoon
15. Spoon
16. Measuring spoons

1 Put all the fruit in the mixing bowl. Add water until the fruit is covered, and let the fruit soak overnight.

2 Have your parents help you bring 1 cup (240 ml) of water and the sugar to a boil in the saucepan. Boil 15 to 20 minutes, stirring constantly until the mixture thickens into a syrup.

3 Add the soaked fruits, nuts, and spices to the syrup. Stir well, let the mixture cool, and refrigerate.

4 Remove cinnamon sticks and serve the chilled khoshaf in glass bowls. Top each serving with a spoonful of yogurt. Enjoy!

GLOSSARY

henna, 21	A red-orange dye made from the leaves of the henna plant.
iftar, 8	The meal eaten after sunset that breaks the fast during Ramadan.
Islam, 4	The religion founded by Prophet Muhammad and defined by the Qur'an.
Ka'bah, 17	A sacred shrine in Mecca at which Muslim pilgrims gather to pray at the beginning and end of the hajj.
lunar, 6	Following the phases of the moon.
mosque, 9	A temple for Islamic worship.
Muslims, 4	Followers of Islam.
pilgrimage, 16	A long journey made for religious reasons.
Qur'an, 8	The holy book of Islam.
revelation, 11	A communication of divine truth; something enlightening revealed by God to humans.
rituals, 16	Traditionally repeated religious acts or ceremonies.
sohour, 9	The meal eaten before sunrise during Ramadan.

INDEX

Picture credits
Kristie Burns: 13 (top), 15 (bottom); Camera Press: 27; Camerapix: 9, 21 (both), 22, 26, 28; Camerapix/COP: 17 (top), 18 (top), 19; Haga Library: 24, 25 (top); HBL Network Photo Agency: 1, 3 (bottom); Hutchison Library: 3 (top); Christine Osborne Pictures: 8 (top), 12, 13 (bottom), 14; Peter Sanders: 2, 4, 6, 8 (bottom), 10, 11, 15 (top), 20, 23 (bottom); Topham Picturepoint: 5; Trip Photographic Library: 7 (both), 16, 17 (bottom), 18 (bottom), 23 (top), 25 (bottom).